SORROW'S

WORDS

WRITING EXERCISES
TO HEAL GRIEF

BY SHEILA BENDER

First Edition, 2013
ISBN 978-1-943224-00-5

Category: 1. Writing and Editing Guide. 2. Counseling and advice services.
I. Author: Bender, Sheila. II. Title: Sorrow's Words: Writing Exercises To
Heal Grief
Writing It Real, 394 Colman Drive, Port Townsend, WA 98368

Table of Contents

Preface
We Need No Barriers

In the month after my son Seth Bender died in a snowboarding accident, I thought that in mourning, I would give up my "best thing," which was writing, because it felt selfish now to write. What was more important than losing my son? How could I write anything worthy of this loss? How could I do anything but sit with my grief, sorrow, and horror—those things we fear and come to believe won't happen to us? Part of sitting with these emotions for me was reading the stories of other parents who had lost their children. They were the people whose company I sought. Experiencing the effects of their writing on me, I began to write about my own son's dying.

As I wrote, I had to learn to live again, now in his memory, with his memory, and with those who had also loved him and those who would have loved him had they known him. Years before Seth died, I had tutored a high school student who told me that after her best friend died, she began to believe that she had to live for two by making her contributions to the world count double. By leaving early, Seth handed me this job. If I were going to heal from this loss, I had to bring his spirit into the world along with mine. I pulled out a postcard he had written home one summer from camp telling us how he was carrying the heaviest load on his bike for his group's campsite and how he was dodging bees as he printed the words on the postcard. That was my son, brave, practical and dedicated. It was not enough that I had given birth to him and that by age 25 he was interested in making contributions to the groups to which he belonged. I would have to contribute more than I might have had he been here. In this way, I could feel his presence with me, in me, around me, and always.

When relatives and writing group members told me that reading my writing about loss helped them through grief of their own and also helped their friends know how to be with them, I decided to finish a book and seek publication. When the development director of our local Marine Science Center interviewed me about the Seth Bender Memorial Camp Scholarships for children that we had begun in Seth's memory, I knew if I did publish the book, I would donate proceeds from its sales to this scholarship fund. I enjoyed the idea that more kids would get to experience the outdoors Seth loved. *A New*

Theology: Turning to Poetry in a Time of Grief came out in 2009. Soon after, I began teaching Writing Grief as a class in-person, to groups, and online, guiding new and experienced writers in what I had done—use the poetry of masters to free my own voice and find the love and beauty that life is, even when anger, hurt, fear, guilt and loneliness clamor for expression.

In *Sorrow's Words: Writing Exercises To Heal Grief,* I hope to inspire you to write from your loss because it will help you know you can survive loss, and in doing so, grow strong, grow deep, and grow in loving. The photographs in Chapter Three as well as the cover photograph are by Port Townsend, WA photographer Sheila Lauder. No stranger to loss, she generously allows me to use her photographs in my writing classes. We hope those we have included here capture feelings not only of loss but of renewal.

Chapter 1
Tell Your Story:
The Outside, The Inside

WHILE I WAS READING ON LOSS, I CAME ACROSS AN INTER-view with shaman Martin Prechtel in the April 2001 issue of *The Sun* magazine. He said that those who have gone before us become our teachers. We must feed them, he said, by metabo-lizing this world with our senses, by being alive to life.

I had always taught students that good writing allows us to use our five senses to experience the world. Even though my son was gone, to write about mourning him, I had to create a world on the page. Writing through loss, I had to evoke him as well as the vacancy I felt now that he was gone. And after loss, the details of my environment become even more vivid. Evoking Seth, I both felt his presence and the loss of his presence. This left me feeling disturbed until I could soothe myself with writing that held him.

Try This #1

Think about the many times you have told the story of your loss. Now write this story. Write the narrative and description of your loss. Then write about your desire to write about the loss and the concerns you have about this kind of writing. All of this is part of what you must explore to discover a way to speak your grief.

Here are some questions to consider as you write:

- What loss are you writing about? Tell as much about it as you want to.
- How long has it been since you suffered the loss?
- What are your hopes for writing about your grief? What are your fears?
- Have you been writing already?
- If you have already been writing, include a passage or two or some lines from that writing that stand out for you now and write about why they do.

- If you haven't begun writing, take some time to write down what you often think about or tell others.

◦◡◦

Sometimes, we put off writing because it seems hard to do, or because we worry we won't write well enough or because what we write might seem more permanent than what we say, more honest, and we are afraid to experience that honesty, especially if it is raw with feeling. But shape emerges in writing and shape helps us heal. When we write, we build homes for our memories and for our feelings, making room inside of ourselves for new memories and for new feelings as we continue our living. We can visit the feeling-homes we've built with our writing any time, and we worry less about forgetting what is important to us. Often, when visiting what we wrote, we witness a beauty we might not have been able at first to see.

I hope I've ignited your desire to write the words sorrow has given you to say.

Chapter 2
Poetry Helps Us Find New Voices

WHEN MY SON DIED, I HAD JUST FINISHED TEACHING THE fall term in the English Department at Loyola Marymount University in Los Angeles. My favorite class was "Poetry for Non-English Majors," for which I used Edward Hirsch's book *How to Read a Poem and Fall in Love with Poetry*. I'd read and re-read the poems in the book; now I began to use them as models to create my own rants, my own chants, out of the sorrow and helplessness in me. I had for weeks been losing my voice, not speaking up, barely speaking above a whisper when I was with others. Using the strategies of these poems, I found first a way to raise my voice ("Do not go gently into that good night," Dylan Thomas pleaded) and then a way to accept the work I had to do.

I envied the words of French poet Robert Desnos in his poem "The Voice of Robert Desnos," included in Hirsch's book. (You can read the entire poem online at Poets.org.) Here is a sample from the poem translated by William Kulik in which Desnos attempts to move a woman he has loved and lost:

> I call to me those lost in the fields
> old skeletons young oaks cut down
> scraps of cloth rotting on the ground and linen
> drying in farm country
> I call tornadoes and hurricanes
> storms typhoons cyclones
> tidal waves
> earthquakes
> I call the smoke of volcanoes and the smoke of
> cigarettes
> the rings of smoke from expensive cigars
> I call lovers and loved ones
> I call the living and the dead

Repeating the phrase "I call" and allowing oneself to direct that call far and wide felt powerful to me. I decided to write an "I call" poem of my own, thanking Robert Desnos for the model:

I Call to the Ski Slopes of Breckenridge After Robert Desnos

I call to the ski slopes of Breckenridge;
I call to the trees on the slopes of Breckenridge;
I call to the snow and the ice hanging in their
    branches;
I call to the snow on the run and the melted layer
    of that snow iced over.
I call to my son, to my son in his thermal clothing,
    to my son,
Twenty-five years old and snowboarding, headed
    into the trees.

I call to my son to tumble off the board and never
    reach the trees.
I call to my son not to worry about looking clumsy,
not to worry about finishing his run.
I call to him and I call.

The ski lift stops with its human
cargo, quiet and still, and trees begin to lean,
but they are slow, and the snow and the ice on
    their boughs
fall in clumps to the ground, batter on a spoon I
    can not see.

My son does not hear me,
but I call over the weeks between then and now
to the hospital and time of death: 3:30 December
    28, 2000,
and he does not tumble where I want him to.

I call clear as the moon, single eye I howl beneath,
    a coyote
licking pebbles from a wound. I call and I call.
    The wound
weeps holy water over my eyelids, hands, knees, feet
that will carry me the rest of my days.

In the snow, I see my sadness crystallize, hear
    my voice
force follicles in my body to burst along their
    single seams,
spread seeds, seeds I see in sunlight and my son
everywhere, everywhere I call.

Using a pattern and strategy inspired by Robert Desnos, I faced my sorrow, powerlessness, and failure as a mother to keep my child from harm in a way that would help me with the next steps in my mourning.

Try This #2

Write a list of places, people, things, and times you might call to. Make the words after "I call" as specific as you can make them. Your title might be simply "I Call" or it might be "The Voice of _____."

Thank Robert Desnos under the title. Thank yourself for allowing the chance to call to the environment you shared with your loved one or the environment in which you lost your loved one.

~⌒~

After I wrote this poem, I decided to write from lines of Walt Whitman's poetry that I had also read and reread since I had taught my class. They are from "Out of the Cradle Endlessly Rocking," a segment in Whitman's book-length poem *Leaves of Grass* (the lines also appear online at Poets.org):

Out of the Cradle Endlessly Rocking by Walt Whitman

Out of the cradle endlessly rocking
Out of the mocking-bird's throat, the musical
    shuttle.

Out of the Ninth-month midnight,
Over the sterile sands, and the fields beyond,
    where the child,
leaving his bed, wander'd alone, bare-headed,
    barefoot,
Down from the shower'd halo,
Up from the mystic play of shadows, twining
    and twisting as if they were alive,
Out from the patches of briers and blackberries,
From the memories of the bird that chanted to me,
From your memories, sad brother—from the fitful
    risings and fallings I heard,
From under that yellow half-moon, late-risen, and
    swollen as if with tears,
From those beginning notes of sickness and love,
    there in the transparent mist,
From the thousand responses of my heart, never
    to cease,
From the myriad thence-arous'd words,
From the word stronger and more delicious than any,
From such, as now they start, the scene revisiting,
As a flock, twittering, rising, or overhead passing,
Borne hither—ere all eludes me, hurriedly,
A man—yet by these tears a little boy again,
Throwing myself on the sand, confronting the waves,

I, chanter of pains and joys, uniter of here and
    hereafter,
Taking all hints to use them—but swiftly leaping
    beyond them,
A reminiscence sing.

A reminiscence sing! That was just the problem. I was
suffering from fear that I was remembering too little about
my son and his life. Whitman's poem fostered the strength
I needed to stop chastising myself for what I feared was too
little to remember compared to how many years Seth was
alive. The poem helped me trust that whatever memories
came were the right ones for me to chant. In the act of chant-
ing, I seemed to sing a resurrection of my boy. I concentrated
on Whitman's ending, reading it and re-reading it, until I felt
I could become a "uniter of here and hereafter," exactly what
I wanted to do.

The memories that came were not from Seth's infancy or
younger years, but from the years he was at the University of
Colorado. I remembered him noticing how out of breath I was
on hikes in that high country when I visited. I saw him taking
off on the trail to scramble up rocks with his step-dad Kurt
and tackling the steepest parts of trails. I heard Seth laughing
at me for not noticing that I was huffing because of the alti-
tude. I remembered how as an upperclassman he meticulously
brewed beer with his roommates. Influenced by Whitman's

poem, I gathered images of Seth that centered on this activity he shared with college friends:

Six months After My Son's Death, I Chant to Sing for Him

Out of daily steps and out of drives
on highways, out of hours' rocky patches
and moments made of weeds, memories come.

I sing the evening I visited my son and watched
his friends working in his kitchen with hops
    and yeast
and recipes downloaded from the Internet.
I sing the carboys they showed me topped
with see-through tubes and shiny copper
for reading yeast's performance.

I sing their logs of sugar content and bottled
batches, the way the young men sterilized the
    bottles
they used, invited people for the harvests
of oatmeal stout and porter. I sing each week
they went to school between their Sunday fests.
Long and deep, I mourn and wake to sing the sun
to rise, to thank my son for time he's spent

inside my dreams. I sing, I sing and do what
he was doing: siphon good spirits from sediment.

Try This #3

See what happens when you allow Whitman's
phrases to inspire you. Begin lines of your own
poetry or prose with those phrases. Finish each of
the lines with details from your life as shared with
the one who is gone, and they will provide a way
for you to resurrect that person's life and spirit.

Another example of a poem that uses the litany form (a list
made by repeating the same words at the opening of lines) is
"We Remember Them," a Jewish prayer for helping those in
mourning honor the ones they have lost. I believe using it as an
example will help you write more about the meaning of your
loved one's life:

We Remember Them

At the rising of the sun and at its going down
We remember them.
At the blowing of the wind and the chill of winter

We remember them.

At the opening of the buds and in the rebirth
   of spring

We remember them.

At the blueness of the skies and in the warmth
   of summer

We remember them.

At the rustling of the leaves and in the beauty
   of autumn

We remember them.

At the beginning of the year and when it ends

We remember them.

As long as we live, they too will live; for they are
   now a part of us, as we remember them.

When we are weary and in need of strength

We remember them.

When we are lost and sick at heart

We remember them.

When we have joy we crave to share

We remember them.

When we have decisions that are difficult to make

We remember them.

When we have achievements that are based on theirs

We remember them.

As long as we live, they too will live; for they are
   now a part of us, as we remember them.

Try This #4

Think of times during the day and year that you remember the one who is gone. Write "I" instead of "we" when you start off each line in a poem like the Jewish prayer. As often as you can, fill in the details of what you are remembering with specifics and tangibles, rather than too frequently using generalities:

> When I go to shop each week for food,
> I remember the way you spied the parking
>   spaces
> even if I were the one driving.
> I think of the way you said, "There's one.
>   Take it."

Details about small moments work very well interspersed with memories more sacred or important. The more specific you are in the details, the more you can make the story of a life you want to hold close.

In his book, *100 Tricks Any Boy Can Do: How My Brother Disappeared*, which is an inquiry into his brother's suicide, author and poet Kim Stafford describes his feeling that writing about his brother has in some ways brought him back to life: "I call this reappearance of my brother 'Bret's last trick,' a stunning, impossible, recurring, and infinitely precious sleight of his hand."

May each of us learn to perform this trick. May each of us find that in writing we find joy despite the tears.

Chapter 3
Visual Art Helps Us Write Grief's Wisdom

WHEN MY SON WAS FIVE, I WROTE A POEM ABOUT BEING in a rowboat with him on Lake Union in Seattle. In the poem, I record his wish that he could "wear his head on backwards for awhile." Rowing on the lake listening to my son brought back my own young school days and childhood fears. But looking at the boat's wake from the point where it began at the stern, brought me back to the present with my son, to knowing I would have to row away from those fears fanning out behind us so I could be the mother I wanted to be.

Twenty years later, a colleague told me she was reading my poems for images about my son. I began doing that as well. I saw that writing from my grief, I had to leave the boat and dive into the wake. I had to cry as I wrote. I had to allow myself to feel the void left where the words had been stored inside of me before I wrote them. I had to become used to the room I would make inside myself for new feelings. I would now write from other snapshot moments that helped me recall my son.

Writing in response to visual art (or to a viewed or remembered scene) produces what is called Ekphrastic writing, a word and a poetic form given to us by the Greeks. According to the Merriam-Webster dictionary, the term means "a literary description" or "commentary on a visual piece of art." The Greek root of the word means "to point out."

You can begin your own Ekphrastic writing by describing exactly what you see in the photographs by Sheila Lauder offered here. Allow your experience with loss to influence how you enter the scene depicted by the photograph. The story you tell may include details that you as a viewer can not actually see but believe are there. You can include events that you imagine came before the photograph's moment or will come later.

Image 3.1 *Armchair by Sheila Lauder*

Here I am
Sitting on a chair, thinking
About you. Thinking
About how it was
To talk to you.

     —Mary Jo Bang "You Were You Are Elegy"

Try This #5

Imagine sitting in the pictured armchair. Write about the way the lamp, the chair, the table and other objects as well as the lighting wait for the person to come back. Write about the memories they hold of the person you miss.

Your passages will reveal what reading the words and looking at the photographs makes you think, makes you remember, compels you to say, pulls out from hiding.

∼⌣∽

In the months after my son died, I took great solace from the sun. From my window, I watched it rise each day, and I went outside to watch it set. Between sunrise and sunset, I read emails with stories about times others had shared with my son. I roamed the condo I lived in. I stood by the television cabinet Seth had climbed atop to fasten a heavy piece of wooden folk art to the wall. I smoothed my hands over the butcher block he sanded. I stared at the pot rack he had fastened to the kitchen ceiling for us. I could see his fingerprints on the chrome. Every piece of furniture, every piece of artwork, even the cats seemed to hold his touch, his care.

After my son died, I sought out books by parents who had lost children and by children who had lost parents. These authors telling their stories were the company I wanted to keep. I could experience my feelings thoroughly by experiencing theirs.

Image 3.2 *The Rain by Sheila Lauder*

Without a listener, the healing process is aborted. Human beings, like plants that bend toward the sunlight, bend toward others in an innate healing tropism. There are times when being listened to is more critical than being fed.

—*Miriam Greenspan,* Healing Through the Dark Emotions: The Wisdom of Grief, Fear, and Despair

Try This #6

If the bird had come to the fence in the rain to think about grief, if this bird were you, what images from the pier would inform thoughts about loss?

What might this bird be thinking, as she carries on normally, though on the inside, she is consumed with feelings of loss and sadness?

You might write as if this is you sitting on the pier in the rain. Or, you might write from the vantage point of the person behind the rain speckled car windshield seeing the bird survive in the elements.

After Seth died, I prayed for a dream in which he would appear to me. Finally, one night, several months after his death, I received that dream. The dream brought peace for me, and I set out to describe the dream and the feelings it brought. I remembered that the villanelle form was used by many poets in grief, Elizabeth Bishop and Thomas Dylan, among them. Here is my poem:

A New Theology
For Seth Bender, 1975-2000

Who has no likeness of a body and has no body
is my son, now five months dead
but in my dreams, my dreams he brings the peace
    in gardens,

and I see him in his smile and he is hardy
in the rolled up sleeves of his new shirt, well-fed
when he has no likeness of a body and has no body.

I see him next to me in conversation at a party
and I believe that he is fine because this is what
    he said,
because in my dreams, my dreams I sit with him
    in gardens.

The nights he comes, the cats moan long and sorry.
I believe they see his spirit entering my head,
he who has no likeness of a body and has no body.
In my life, accepting death comes slowly,
but the midwifery of sadness and of shock bleeds
afterbirth, dreams that bring the peace in gardens.

I know that he is far and he is here and he is holy.
Under sun, I feel the energy it takes to come away
    from God
who has no likeness of a body and has no body
who is in my dreams, the dreams that bring me
    gardens.

After the first memorial service held for my son just days after he'd died, I'd spoken with Richard, a social worker who was Seth's neighbor in Berkeley, CA. He, like many who were close to Seth in Northern California, rushed to the services we held in Seattle, where Seth had grown up. Richard was a good listener, and he had talked about many things with Seth that fall and winter as Seth was deciding on marriage and a job change. I told Richard about premonitions I had had over the past months that my son's life was coming to an end, things I hadn't said to anybody. Richard told me that the kind of fatigue I was interpreting was that of a young man who was making important life decisions. But a month later, at a second memorial service, this time in Berkeley, Richard told me about a dream he'd had in which Seth said, "My mom is right." This sounded just like my son. He'd always spoken succinctly about important things. I felt he was correcting Richard's social worker explanation, and I was grateful.

Image 3.3 *Rain Circles by Sheila Lauder*

Our dreams interpenetrate. Sometimes we even find that the dream we thought we had lost is alive in someone else, who can return it to us.

—*Rabbi David J. Wolpe,* Making Loss Matter: Creating Meaning in Difficult Times

It seems again that dreams, not reason, are the friends of those who grieve.

—*Sheila Bender,* A New Theology: Turning to Poetry in a Time of Grief

33

Try This #7

Look at the image of rain circles on water. Think of the circles as representing dreams. Reflect on the idea that dreams might carry meaning across boundaries.

If you've been told by someone else about a dream in which your loved one had a message for you, received such a dream yourself about your beloved or someone else's departed, write about this.

Even if you have not received this kind of information, imagine who or what might bring a dream about the departed to you. The wind, the highest tree, the tender seedling, the family of deer that visits your yard, a head of dandelion seeds? Invite that place, person, memory into your writing. Ask for the dream and its message. Write it down.

～◡～

Here are some lines from Kim Stafford's book, *100 Tricks Every Boy Can Do: How My Brother Disappeared*, to inspire more writing. He is remembering his brother during family journeys. It was, Stafford writes, as if he were asking, "Can I always love what I once held close?"

He seemed to fancy journeys. He loved maps, bought himself a little implement you could adjust for scale and roll across a map to learn the exact distance from one place to another. There is something in the family's yo-yo rhythm of migration that prefigures my brother's later pattern of traveling in search of independence and then returning home in search of security.

In one of our early migrations, when we left Iowa for Oregon again, little Bret wistfully asked, as he surveyed the new place, "Does our sky hook onto Donna's sky?

Image 3.4 *Along the Trail by Sheila Lauder*

*If he could be alive again, taste huckleberries on
this trail, and stand together with a kind friend,
what might he want?*

—*Kim Stafford,* 100 Tricks Every Boy Can Do:
How My Brother Disappeared

 **Try This #8**

Although as viewers we can't see the faces of the
two cyclists along the trail, as writers we can imagine their expressions, what they might be thinking
as they look at the sky and if they are talking to one
another. Perhaps you imagine one of them as yourself and the other as someone who also loved the
departed; or perhaps you can imagine the beloved
being somewhere in the scene, as cyclist or para-
sailor, as smoke or the path, for instance.

Alternately, you can imagine the figures in the photograph as parts of yourself in this time of adapting
to loss. What story might each be remembering in
his or her own way while looking at the spectacle
in the sky?

In your writing, associate from the details in the photograph to details from your experience with your loved one or let your loved one speak as he or she parasails before you.

～⌒

Your emotions and associations will infuse your words as you concentrate on the details in the stories each tells from the trail. In those details, you will discover that the one who is gone has a voice inside you with lessons and messages to relay.

Image 3.5 *Heart Rock by Sheila Lauder*

So the darkness shall be the light, and the stillness the dancing.

—*T.S. Eliot,* "East Coker" Four Quartets

 **Try This #9**

Concentrate on the image of the heart rock as you think about an object you would choose. It will remind you that inanimate objects carry the emotions of your heart.

Write a few paragraphs in which you take this object to a specific place with which you are familiar. Describe the place you are imagining. What do you see, feel, taste, touch and smell in this location? What can you say of the ground and the air, the time of year? Is it dry or wet? Is the sun out or are there clouds? Are there trees or fences, flowers or seashells? What do you carry with you to this burial?

Write about why you chose the particular object you did to bury. Write about the ceremony you will perform, the way you will lay the object in its resting place. Write about what you feel now that you have buried it.

The heart rock shines through clear water. Like this image, our memories and love need not be obscured. They can shine in relief against the scalloped sediment of loss.

One way to do this in writing is to imagine that you are burying something associated with your loss, something you don't really want to bury but will think about for this writing exercise: an article of clothing, a particular gift, a book, a cooking utensil, a notebook, a briefcase, a CD—it can be anything that you associate with the one who is now gone.

Here is writing from Susan Bellfield, who chose to write about burying her mother's ashes:

> The brutal Chicago wind seems to pass through me. I am a ghost to the city I abandoned twenty years ago. My breath fogs the air and dissipates toward the leaden sky. It will snow today, blanketing the grimy streets in pristine white to temporarily fool the eye and heart into believing in beauty, goodness and hope.
>
> I recall the promise; the weight of my shoulder bag will not allow me to forget. Five pounds is a dubious measure of a lifetime of struggle, joy, and love. But uncertainty causes me to defer, to wander off course.
>
> Attracted by children's shouts I pause to watch a game of scrimmage in the overgrown lot serving

as a park. The pass is fumbled and several of the larger boys fall onto the loose ball. As the struggle for control subsides I can see that the ball has split open. Disappointed, the children slowly disperse. I rest my head against the buckled fence and release tears of hazy origin. Am I crying for children who play in makeshift fields? Am I weeping because joy is so quickly replaced with disappointment and sorrow? Is my grief identification with the deflated ball, both of us bereft of the buoyancy and support that permits us to soar?

The snow begins to fall in great clumps, deadening my footsteps and muting the din of the city as I turn north to negotiate the final two blocks of my journey.

I pass shops and houses, each festooned with colored lights, garlands and twinkling trees, but my heart refuses to acknowledge the joy of the season. This was her favorite holiday. She would start the day after Thanksgiving by dressing every inch of the house in Christmas, sweetening the air with enough baked goods to feed fifty families, and amassing gifts as if her wallet was on fire. And because she made the holiday so magical for us all, it used to be my favorite too. Now it is only another reminder of her absence, another day to fill with meaningless activity.

It has taken me three hours to walk six blocks to the place where she cheered with her father. The home of the team she taught her husband to love. The place she ate hot dogs with her children and sang 'Take Me Out to the Ballgame'. The place where she joked that sprinkling her ashes would break the curse of the goat.

The stadium appears abandoned. There is no baseball in December. Mom would have known that and maybe, just maybe, so did I. I'm not ready to lose her, to give her to the world. I need to keep her close so I don't forget her voice, her smile, her embrace, her steadfast belief in my goodness and perfection despite my obvious flaws.

Maybe in the spring...

Image 3.6 *On The Moor by Sheila Lauder*

*I wake to sleep, and take my waking slow. I learn by
going where I have to go.*
— *Theodore Roethke,* "The Waking"

Looking at the photograph of the man and his dog on the
moor, I remember teaching in the mountains of Colorado a
year and a half after my son's death. In my sorrow, I began, with
the help of a website, to name the wild flowers around me there:

> Columbine, Aquilegia vulgaris, aquilegus a Latin
> adjective meaning "drawing water," spurs where the
> flower nectar collects. Lupine, Lupinous perennis,
> from the Latin lupus ("wolf"), once thought to
> deplete or "wolf" the mineral content of soil, actually
> enhances soil fertility by fixing atmospheric nitrogen
> into a useful form. Turkish blue, Veronica liwanensis,
> groundcover that may appear fragile but is tough,
> grows well in full sun among other plants and
> between paving stones, and on rock walls, equally at
> home along the Front Range and at 10,000 feet.

I realize now how details fix the atmospheric minerals of
mourning into the ground we walk on, into the ground that
will foster beautiful blossoms for our spirit.

I went on writing then, thinking about my new grandson
Toby, as well as my son, who was no longer here. Eventually,

these two questions occurred to me: "How can I not look at the pain of losing him? But how can I not look to the future?"

And I wrote on:

> Toby is the first of a new generation descended from me. May he always find water to quench his thirst, dew on green leaves to make him smile. May he find what he needs in the air and in the stars. May he grow in full sun, amidst family and many fine friends, as a small boy starting out, as a man taller than his mother.

Try This #10

As you contemplate the image of the man on the moor, think about what place in nature suits your feelings since your loss. You can use the landscape in this photograph of the moors, if you wish to. Whether you use the photo's landscape, one you've visited, or one with which you are very familiar, write as if you are looking over this landscape. Name what you see and those details will lead you to the questions mourning has raised.

Chapter 4
Writing Letters Helps Us Find Lost Parts of Ourselves

IN THE WEEKS AFTER SETH DIED, WE RECEIVED NUMEROUS notes from his friends that recounted memorable times they had shared with Seth. Each of these notes helped us believe that although he'd lived only to 25, memories of him would keep his spirit alive. I soon found postcards Seth had sent us when he was at summer camp, and I framed them because the messages he'd written helped me remember the way he spoke. Of course, I had the urge many times to phone him, email him, call out to him as if he were visiting us, and I could tell him what his friends and I remembered of his life.

Kurt remembers how after Seth's death, we talked not only of wanting to add to our memories of him, but also how in losing him, we felt we had also lost the parts of ourselves he brought out in us, the parts alive in his memories. I believe that writing letters to the one who has departed can restore both their spirit to us and the spirit they treasured in us.

Writing letters to those who are no longer here offers the opportunity to feel listened to as the one we love would have listened. It allows us to reflect on what parts of ourselves we want our beloved to know and to think about. It helps us feel known and loved and loving.

Try This #11

Sit somewhere that allows you to remember your loved one and write a letter. Begin by describing this place you are sitting—what you see and feel, taste, touch, and hear in this spot. Next, focus on a specific memory that comes to you as you sit. Write it into the letter as if you are sharing it with your loved one. After you have written the memory, write about why you think you are thinking of this memory now in the place where you are sitting and writing.

Next, add in information about your days now—
scenes from books you are reading, writing you
have done, movies you've seen, places you've gone
or people who have done something meaningful
recently. As you near the end of your letter, see if
there is something the person you are addressing
would find important to know about you right
now. State what it is.

~‿⁀

This writing exercise can be bold and direct or subtle as in
these paragraphs by Karin Goldberg:

Dear Mother,

I am sitting in my office. It is in the second
bedroom of our loft. I have a large screen monitor
and a good desktop computer. There are many
books and CD's that I haven't tidied up and the
whole place is kind of a mess, but it's my mess and
my place to write. The walls are apartment white,
but since this is a loft in a converted shoe factory,
they are 13 feet high. Lots of space, lots of freedom
to write about my family, my history, my present.
Behind me I've newly installed our old sofa. It's a
welcome addition to my creative cave. There isn't

any natural light in here; the large concrete beam blocks out the light that comes from one bank of windows in the living room. It's funny because the beam looks like a large flashlight but I haven't been able to find the switch.

In here, I write about my losses, my anger, my grief and my joy. I write about my sons and the most excellent lives that they are living. But sometimes, I write about feeling neglected, something that has surprised me. The older my boys get—boys? they are adults—the more I feel the need to spend time with them. It's not to make up for the time that I lost with them, but that I just want their company. I want to know that I mean something to them.

When Michael was born, my in-laws came to stay with us. As you know, I liked my mother-in-law. One day she was standing just outside of the living room where I was holding my son, looking at the baby in my arms, looking into his dark eyes that were looking up into mine as I asked, "Do you love me?" She entered the room and I looked up, embarrassed and she said, "Of course he loves you, you're his mother." But don't mothers have to earn love? I don't know, because I am not sure that I am a real mother.

These are issues that I'm still working out in my writing and in this office as I listen to classical music and old time radio shows. Shows that people listened to in the past when there was no television.

And even as I'm waiting to feel sleep overtake me, I listen to these shows on my iPod, mystery shows, comedy, and I imagine the actors reading their scripts into old microphones with their round and ugly presence, so much different from our electronics of today. Soon, I will take the ear buds out, place my iPod on my night table and sleep.

In my dream, I will not know this house. I am inside though; it is a larger house than I grew up in. Dad comes in. I am delighted to see him. He looks so well. He's wearing a dark brown suit and a robin's egg blue tie that matches his eyes. I call him Daddy which is odd because I know that I am 62 years old. I am living in your house. You have taken me in and let me live with you. I am lost. I have no job, and keep going back to school but obstacle after obstacle prevents me from finishing my course work.

Sometimes, I don't even get to start because I can't find the right textbooks. I know that I should move out; I'm not even paying rent, but you cook for me and allow me my space. I get angry with you though I realize how good it is that you have let me live here. I don't know what I am going to do with my life, which at 62 and still living at home has been stunted.

I wake up from a fitful sleep.

I love you, Mom,
Karin

 Try This #12

During another writing time, choose a spot you shared with the one who is gone. Plan to write another letter in separate sittings over the course of a day or a week or a month.

- The first time you go there, write a letter from now, this time after your loss. Describe where you are sitting and how what you see and hear, taste, touch and smell from there inspires you to write to the deceased.
- The second time, write a letter from a time before the loss. Use something in the environment where you are sitting to let your loved one know why you are inspired to write about this time before your loss.

- The third time, write a letter about how you imagine the future now that your loved one is not here to share in living it.
- After the letters are written, figure out in which you order you feel you might best present the letters to the recipient and write the recipient about why you are thinking of arranging them in the order you have chosen.

~⌣⌐

Another idea to help you write a letter to your loved one is to use a metaphor to describe the loved one and their place in your life. In "The Queen" by Pablo Neruda, the poet notes:

> No one sees your crystal crown, no one looks
> At the carpet of red gold
> That you tread as you pass,
> The nonexistent carpet.

Even so, his beloved is to him a queen and when she is near, he writes:

> All the rivers sound
> In my body, bells
> Shake the sky...

Try This #13

You can adopt Neruda's strategy in a letter you write to your beloved departed. You might want to begin your letter with the phrase, "I call you...."

What might you name your loved one? It can the name of a bird, a kind of food you eat each day that nourishes you, a specific flower or sound or piece of furniture. Let yourself associate to something that seems very right to you and tell the person to whom you are writing your letter what the metaphor is and why it fits. If nothing comes to mind right away, take a look, as I did, at the meaning of the person's name—you might find the metaphor.

~ ~

Here is a letter I wrote to Seth using a metaphor that helped me find meaning:

Dear Seth,

These days, I find myself calling you "sun boat" after a Greek myth I read recently when I looked up the meaning of your name (something

I am not sure I ever did, even when your father and I selected that name for you). In the myth, a hero Seth has the job of keeping the sun from disappearing. The story goes that the dragon Apophis would from time to time devour the Sun Boat of Ra as it sailed the skies. When Apophis swallowed the boat, Seth and a friend had to cut a hole in his stomach to keep the world from being plunged into darkness.

Losing you plunged me into darkness, but somehow the sun rises and it sets and it calls to me each day—as I watch it rise and watch it set, I know you are the "son" boat who cuts the hole through which light and poetry arrive. I am so grateful, Seth, as Ra must have been to his Seth.

With love,
Your Mom

 **Try This #14**

For more letter writing, try this exercise in which you will write both a letter to the departed and their answer to it:

First, choose a place to write from that your loved one had never sat with you. As you write, describe this place by letting your letter's recipient know what you see, hear, taste, touch and smell. Is there a message that arises out of your description of your now? After you write the message, go on to write why it is important for you to write this message now in this letter to your loved one. When you are finished, sign off with something from your feelings at the moment—"With tears and smiles," for instance, or "I look for your smile everywhere."

Next, right after you've finished the first letter and from this same place, think of your loved one somewhere nearby in the same setting— outside a window, in the garden beyond the deck where you sit, perched on the counter top in your kitchen, for instance—writing a letter to you.

Begin their letter to you by having them write about noticing an article of clothing you are wearing. Let them write to you about why they are noticing it and what it means to them about you.

Then keep writing their letter to you until their message to you arises; you will learn what they want you to know.

〜✑〜

You might mail this letter to yourself and when it arrives, hold it in your hand. How tangible the knowledge this person brings.

Here is a brief exchange Steve Blair wrote in one of my classes:

Hi Dad,

I'm going to the Jefferson County transfer station today, the dump. I have to recycle plastic, glass, and paper. It would be more fun if you were with me and we could laugh if the wind were just right and we got a whiff of the garbage nearby.

The sun's out and the heat is warm on the back of my neck.

I'll do this again in two weeks,
Steve

Hi Steve,

I see you're wearing jeans & flip-flops. You must be having a nice day in the sunshine. Watch

out for the bees. I hope you have your EpiPen
handy! Have you gone sailing or flying lately?
    You sure have a nice house. I love the view.

See you in a couple of weeks,
Dad

Whether you write short (postcard length) or you write
long, this kind of correspondence is a wonderful way to
keep the departed current about your life and have them be
with you.

Chapter 5
Fully Alive

EVERY YEAR ON DECEMBER 27, THE ANNIVERSARY OF OUR son's fatal snowboarding accident, Kurt and I head to where we can watch the sunrise. One year, we walked across a narrow road to a long pier. Below us, the water seemed to me to be undulating in an unusual pattern and rhythm, almost like the backs of dolphins. Walking to our car, I asked if he saw anything in the water, and he described being mesmerized by an unusual motion. He said the movement did not seem to correspond with any wave action or tidal currents. I feel certain that what we witnessed was there for us because of the change in our beings on this day, our heightened sense of belonging to a whole, the sense that allows us to locate Seth, to fully feel his presence.

In grief, we perceive the world differently, more personally. To me, it is as if creation wants us to know that we are part of something large and beautiful, and that if we allow this meaning in, peace arrives.

The snippets of perception and time that arise in our writing are part of what can help us perceive that whole. In writing from loss, we evoke our anger, our fear, and our sorrow and learn, I think, that grief is another door to love.

 **Try This #15**

There are several ways to use the writing you have done since your loss to find that door.

Look through your writing and find five or so of your most often repeated words. Choose three of them that carry the most charge for you right now, and write a passage or two under each of those three words. After you've written under the words, make a list of three things you can say about yourself with conviction after writing from your associations with these words. Can you think of a title for the whole of this writing in parts (each with one of the words as a subtitle)? Perhaps, "Now" will turn out to be a good title.

Another way to create a whole from snippets is to honor what editor Olivia Dresher calls the genre of "fragmentary writing." Here are excerpts from "Moments & Confessions," her contribution to the anthology *In Pieces:*

> January 14
> Sometimes everything seems off
> and all the world around me begins to tilt.

> January 15
> The relief of watching the birds
> just that

> January 16
> The wind remembers

> March 17th
> My mind is a tornado in my heart
> My heart is a tornado in my mind

> November 2
> What are my fragments?
> Parachutes that open as I fall through the night.

Here are results from when I recently tried my hand at this style of recording perception:

Grief's Moments

I.
The moon is in partial eclipse.
Where do I find the light of loved ones,
those here and those already gone?

II.
In a recent dream, I walked
from my bedroom to the living room
and outside the window saw a large
coyote sitting in our deck rocking chair.
The animal ran from the chair
into our garden as I approached
the window glass. When I decided
to turn away, he came back.

III.
My son at five or so telling his dad to give
him some elbow grease so he could
do a good job helping his grandmother clean.

IV.
Been in the garden today, pruning boysenberry vines.
Sweet plumb berries, harsh thorns, green, green leaves.

Try This #16

Write down phrases and short passages informed by where you are or what you are thinking and feeling since your loss. Try for specifics from nature and your surroundings. Include snippets of overheard conversation or things people say that you store in your ears and heart for whatever reasons. Number these phrases. Give the list of them a title like the ones in the examples or like "Since You Are Gone."

Whether you write in lines of poetry or prose passages, in one sitting or over days, you can find your experience of being alive, what keeps you present to the world, the richness you contribute, and the richness life contributes to you.

❧

Chapter 6
Continuing

EVERY YEAR FROM SETH'S BIRTHDAY (OCTOBER 1) THROUGH Thanksgiving (the last visit we had before his accident a month later) and then through December 28th (when life support stopped), my sorrow rises like a tide inside and brings an intensity to the sadness I carry each day along with the joy and pleasure I also have in my daughter and her family, my mother, who has come to live close to where I live, my husband, who shares his memories of Seth with me, and my work, through which I facilitate people's writing. Some years, I think I will be too busy to feel the tide and that worries me. I don't want to forget. I want to remember everything about my son. I want to find a way always to make this loss matter.

I find I don't have to worry, because even if I am not paying attention, the tide carries me out (more gently each year) into the thoughts I need to find, and, if I allow myself to write, it will carry me back to the shore gently, too. The exercises I share are part of my approach to writing and are always there for me as strategies, even when I don't set about to strictly follow them.

If you want to continue writing, you can do the exercises again any time and you will get different results. And like me, you may find that whenever you write, the practice you've had with the exercises exerts its influence.

Here is a letter I wrote at the end of November, 2012, almost 12 years after Seth's accident, when I was awakened way too early:

Dear Family, Dear Friends,

This weekend, I awoke suddenly from sleep at two AM and tried my best to stay still and fall back asleep, to not wake Kurt, but I was very restless. I slipped out of bed and walked carefully through the dark hallway to the living room. 'Twas the night after shopping all day in box stores and in the dim light that came from our front windows, I saw the Costco million-packs of toilet paper, paper towels and tissues sitting on our couch, the economy size box of space-saving storage bags on the seat of my favorite chair.

Jars of Trader Joe's almond butter and bottles
of grade B (Kurt's favorite) maple syrup took
up the kitchen counter; boxes and cellophane
bags of more staples nestled in grocery sacks on
the floor. When you drive two and a half hours
round trip to the stores, you want each excursion
to be one you don't have to repeat very often.

I wanted to yell out to the clutter, "Can you
stow yourselves away, stow away all?" Why had
we told ourselves we'd have the energy for sorting
and storing in the morning? I didn't need one
more thing to do the next day. But cleaning up
in our little house would wake Kurt, so I settled
with my laptop into my second-choice chair and
began to think about things out of place.

I had instigated bathroom remodels this
spring and with nowhere to store materials,
the contractor had taken over one of our two
bedrooms. Having to move furniture to make
room for his materials and his tools, he needed
me to empty a tall armoire full of linens and
towels. For months, the colorful cloth of our
lives resided on the living room couch in a pile
Kurt called our Turkish bazaar since he'd come
with our group of writers to Istanbul in May
and the images of that colorful city remained

vivid. All of June, July, August and September, our front door was open to provide ventilation for the men tearing down walls and putting them back up, wiring for new spaces, and laying down tile. With the door open they also had one fewer thing to handle as they came in and went out. Flies flew in widening circles over boxes of toilets, sinks, faucets, lighting fixtures and a bathtub. When Kurt had an emergency abdominal appendectomy and a week later was released from the hospital, we began sleeping in our offices, which are connected by a tiny bathroom not involved in the remodel, Kurt in a reclining chair we'd gotten from Habitat for Humanity to keep him from tossing and turning and disrupting the incision and me on a sofa bed with a memory foam topper. We called to one another, "Good night, Baby, sleep tight," "Do you need anything?" "Yes, maybe some water."

During the months of our things and ourselves out of place–bags of items from vanity drawers in a corner by my dresser, maple doors lining the wall behind Kurt's dresser, summer plans not happening when we'd wanted them to—a cancelled trip to visit Kurt's widowed father and join in a class reunion—I grew restless about restoring order, about exerting control where I could. My closet and drawers are neater now than ever. I weeded through Kurt's jeans and his shirts, making trips to Goodwill. I sorted through forgotten keys, discarding ones that open none of our doors. Once Kurt healed, we dusted and vacuumed and vacuumed and dusted and dusted and vacuumed. At five feet tall, I took in the floors and tables, and at six-foot-three, Kurt concentrated his efforts on the tops of our cabinets and high shelves, both of us grateful for his recovery.

You can't tell at night or on the gray days of our rainy season, but our windows sorely need washing and the window coverings need cleaning, too. (Did you know that flies, caught between the shades and the window glass poop little brown dots?)

It is impossible to have remodeling happening in the center of a small house and not have the whole house involved, not only in the event but in its aftermath. Is the desired result worth the turmoil of getting there? Thankfully, we are happy with our new shower, which Kurt has named the Carnegie shower because its acoustics for singing are the best he's ever experienced in a bathroom. Our new guest bathroom has room for a tub and has an entrance more discreet than the original. But every time I walk to that new entrance, retrace a walkway different than the one my son Seth (who aspired to become an architect) designed for our built-on-a-tight-budget house, I feel what is missing, what will never be the same. I relive his sudden death eight years after he designed the house; I also feel the bittersweet dynamics of our lives going on. Up to now, I could not bring myself to paint a new color on the walls of this home. I needed everything as it was to feel my boy with me.

When my mother came recently to see the finished bathrooms, she said: "Seth would like what you did very much." Of course, my mother gave me a gift by saying what I had hoped would be true, the influence of my son spreading into the new tributaries that flow from the place we once shared.

I thought of how Seth's nature reinforced mine—we shared a love of putting in the energy necessary for a desired effect and enjoyed creating order in what surrounded us. I thought about those traits and how they became hallmarks of his way of life and of his work as an architect. I realized again how deep my wish was all these months to have been able to consult with him about the changes to "his" house, even via dreams, if he would come. Then, I remembered a very recent dream in which I walked this same walk from bedroom to living room. Outside the window, a large coyote was sitting comfortably in our deck rocking chair. As I approached the window glass, the animal ran quickly into the garden. I turned from the glass and he came back, taking his comfortable seat on the chair. Sitting in the living room remembering that dream, I wondered if there was a message I could interpret as coming from Seth and remembered how after the house was done, I asked him for help with landscaping choices, but he left those choices all up to me.

The rocking chair was empty, of course, this night as I sat amidst the shopping clutter. But I realized having dreamed him, the coyote will always be there for me, reminding me that my strength is in living and that my son is in his fleeting way here as well; with every glimpse of him, among the old and among the new, I am renewed.

I looked again at the disarray of items in my living room. Keeping order or allowing disorder, keeping things the same or changing them, either way offers us a look into our lives. As December approaches and for my family, the 12th anniversary of Seth's death, I am grateful to live in this house he designed, grateful to have been able to update it, grateful for Kurt's quick recovery, and grateful for the coyote who draws me from sleep to the stillness where essences mingle.

In the morning, Kurt and I would again dust the laundry room and pantry shelves and then put all the shopping away. For now, I was ready for sleep.

My love,
Sheila

Continuing to write the truth of feelings and perceptions takes courage, and it is difficult at times to truly honor our writing as essential when there are so many tasks and people requiring our attention. Additionally, when it comes to writing about truths and memories, we might all too often judge our own writing as inconsequential.

Nothing is further from the truth. Discovering our truths in words, listening to ourselves, as we would have another listen, heals. It creates intimacy both within us and, if we share the writing, with others. Intimacy is something without which we can not feel fully human. Intimacy is something those of us who have lost loved ones need to continue feeling. We write to express ourselves; in doing so, we nurture intimacy and the feeling that others in our world, both here and gone, matter. I have written these affirmations to help us remember how important writing is:

Acknowledging

That we write because we feel the need,
That we write because we want to reflect on the
meaning in our experience,
That we write because we want to get something
down for others to read after we are gone,
That we write because we are alive and writing
makes us more alive,
That we write because it is a form of play,
That we write because it brings us into contact
with other writers whose minds and hearts
we resonate with,
That we write because it makes us the people we
want to be
Makes writing the gift we cannot refuse to accept.

Please, please keep writing.

Acknowledgments

Like with all writing projects, the end result is heightened by the generosity of many. I would like to thank my first readers Beth Bacon and Kurt VanderSluis for comments they offered after reading early drafts of this book. Telling me what they longed for that wasn't yet written helped me bring the project I'd dreamed of to fruition.

I want to also thank Brenda Miller for her confidence in this book and Christi Killien for her belief in the work and her very close editing eye on the final draft. Sheila Lauder, your generosity in sharing your photos with my classes and in this book have made the working relationship of writers to their words ever more versatile. To those who have studied with me and shown me how these exercises work, my deepest thanks.

A special thank you to Steve Blair, Karin Goldberg, and Susan Bellfield for their permission to use their exercise results as examples in Chapter Five. And I offer many thanks to my daughter, Emily Bender, and her family for the use of their home as a writing retreat while they were away and for the many bars of healthy dark chocolate stacked with a note encouraging inspiration as I tackled the drafting.

About The Author

Sheila Bender is the founder and publisher of WritingItReal.com, an organization whose mission is to facilitate writing from personal experience. She has worked with hundreds of people helping them write personal essays, poetry, flash nonfiction, and meaningful journals. She has served as Distinguished Guest Lecturer at Seattle University and teaches regularly at writer's conferences across the United States.

Imago Press published her memoir, *A New Theology: Turning to Poetry in a Time of Grief*, and a collection of her poems, *Behind Us the Way Grows Wider*. Her first book about writing, *Writing In A Convertible With The Top Down*, co-authored with Christi Killien has recently been re-issued by Writing It Real. *Creative Writing Demystified* is available from McGraw-Hill.
Visit WritingItReal.com to learn about her all of Sheila's books and instructional writing and to contact her.
Visit facebook.com/writingitreal and facebook.com/anewtheology for postings on writing and on surviving grief.

About the Photographer

Sheila Lauder is a retired television production script supervisor. She began her career in the United Kingdom working in daily news and ended her career working on the series *Friends* in Los Angeles.

A member of her local Port Townsend, Washington photography club, she has won many awards for her photography at Jefferson county photography exhibitions.

In 2008, Sheila traveled to New York City to view her photograph, Rocky's Nose, which had been chosen as a winner in Kodak's Picture of the Day contest and then displayed for 24 hours on their enormous Time Square billboard as well as on their website.

Over the years, Sheila has captured thousands of images. She continues to find pictures everywhere.

Praise for Sorrow's Words

Sorrow's Words *is a beautiful, wise, tender, and compassionate book. Sheila Bender guides us in writing during our most vulnerable hours. She does so with both a strong and gentle touch, and she introduces us to many allies who can help us as we face loss and live on.*

—*Brenda Miller,* author of Blessing of the Animals *and co-author of* The Pen and The Bell: Mindful Writing in a Busy World

When poet, essayist and writing teacher Sheila Bender suffered the unimaginable—losing her son Seth in a snowboarding accident—she contemplated giving up writing, her "best thing," to

honor the loss. Thankfully, she reconsidered and instead opened her heart, sharing her own words of sorrow and teaching others to give voice to their deepest grief. Sorrow's Words *is the result of this brave decision and the reader would be wise to heed her words. In this concise, clear volume, Bender demonstrates how to embrace the healing power of grief. Using poems from Whitman and Neruda, visual images—"like this image, our memories and love...can shine in relief against the scalloped sediment of loss"— she invites us to re-enter dreams and revisit familiar landscapes, encouraging us with poignant examples from her own poems and journals. Bender knows this difficult terrain well and offers readers a sure path through it, gently showing that "grief is another door to love."* Sorrow's Words *is a valuable companion to anyone who's suffered loss, and an eloquent reminder of the power of words to witness and heal.*

—Holly J. Hughes, editor of Beyond Forgetting: Poetry and Prose about Alzheimer's Disease *and co-author of* The Pen & The Bell: Mindful Writing in a Busy World

I read Sheila's book and it is wonderful. I've actually used some of these strategies in my work helping people express grief. It's true that writing and having our words witnessed by others can be a safe place to feel our grief and know that we're not alone. I love how Sheila encourages us to read the master poets to help inspire our own writing. And, I really like how she teaches strategies that poets have used...."I call" and "I sing" and returning to nature... and showing it in her own poetry. She teaches us to trust the writing process as a way to find meaning again and to live fully with our losses.

—*Leslie Overturf, Grief Support Counselor, MA Counseling Psychology*

This book will inspire expressive writing and deeper acceptance of the journey of loss for many readers over time.

—*Dr. Jacquelyn Bell, Licensed Psychologist*

CPSIA information can be obtained
at www.ICGtesting.com
Printed in the USA
FSOW02n1246120216
16878FS